Jay

Dear Val and Eldon —
Some light reading for your trip home to Tulsa.
With affection,
Jack

Bugs Us All

Bugs Us All

Poems by Scot Slaby

Drawings by Walter Gurbo

ENTASIS PRESS

WASHINGTON, D.C.

Published by
ENTASIS PRESS
WASHINGTON, D.C.
2016

ISBN 978-0-9850997-4-9

Poems Copyright 2016 by Scot Slaby
Drawings Copyright 2016 by Walter Gurbo

All rights reserved. No part of this publication may be reproduced, stored in a retrieval system, or transmitted, in any form or by any means, without the prior written permission of the publisher. Printed in China.

For my kids, Ella and Walt.
　　　　　Scot Slaby

For Tomoko and Tak.
　　　　　Walter Gurbo

Contents

Do the Spiders 1
This Ant 2
A Peek 3
At the School 4
Jarflies 5
Trespassing 6
Mantis 7
Bug from the Drain 8
Swimming 11
Honey Bee 12
A Pantry 13
Coat-of-Arms 14
Flit, Dip, and Glide 15
Assassin Bugs 16
Wanderlust 17
Resting 19
The Thinker 20
Back Alley 21
Jesus Bugs 22
The Centipede 24
Odiferous 25
The Date 26
Reading 27
Dusk 28

Bugs Us All

Do the spiders that live in this room
keep reminding you of your own doom?
Put your feet up and read.
They're not waiting to feed,
so relax and try not to assume.

While this ant can't move well, his persistence
permits him to travel great distance.
Death hasn't yet gobbled
(despite being hobbled)
This old bug who needs some assistance.

It's clear
that the reason
I'm cowering
is a bug
has been watching
me showering.
He's been
sneaking
a peek
of my
naked
physique!
But for him,
voyeurism's
empowering.

At the school, all the head lice are browsy
as they move to the neat from the frowzy.
The nurse found some nits,
which is why one kid sits
in the health room. Are his parents lousy?

In the jarflies'
 safe underground lair,
like the Morlocks,
 they wait and prepare
for their brood's
 insurrection—
their swarm's
 resurrection—
when their operas
 will rattle the air!

When you've trespassed and you're apprehended,
and the property owner's offended,
you can't worm your way out
since his sign left no doubt:
underground, rights to roam aren't defended.

The bulbous green part of this plant is
no plant but the eyes of a mantis!
Is his deep meditation
a sincere supplication?
Leave him be to be more like Saint Francis.

I'm afraid of you,
bug from the drain.
Will you crawl through my ear
to my brain?
Your abdominal pincher
looks like it could injure,
so it's time for my full
coup de main!

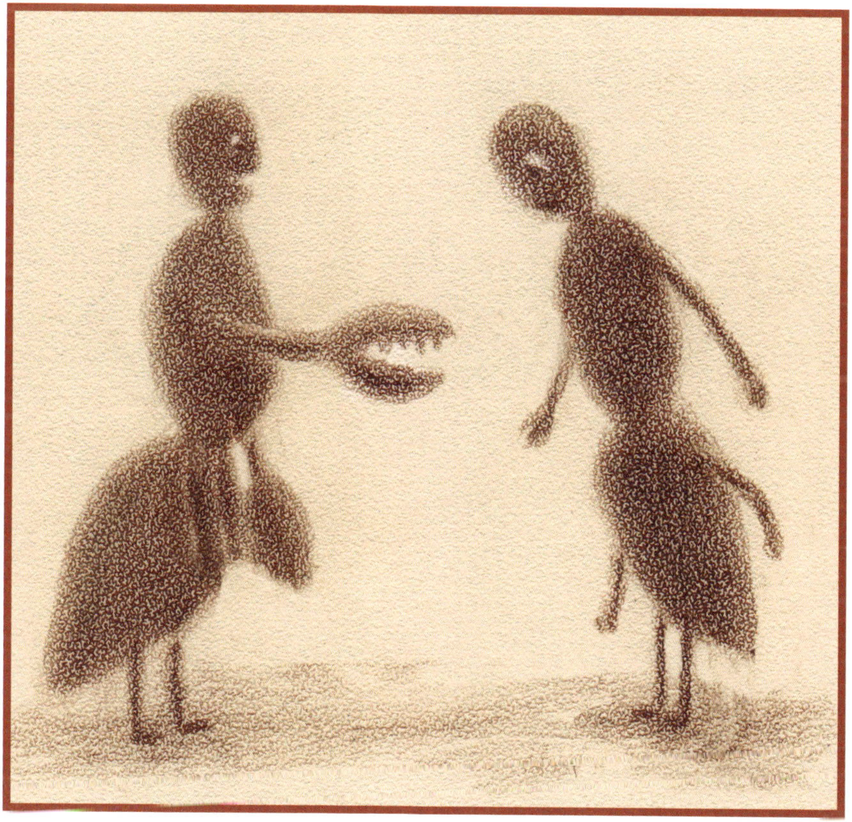

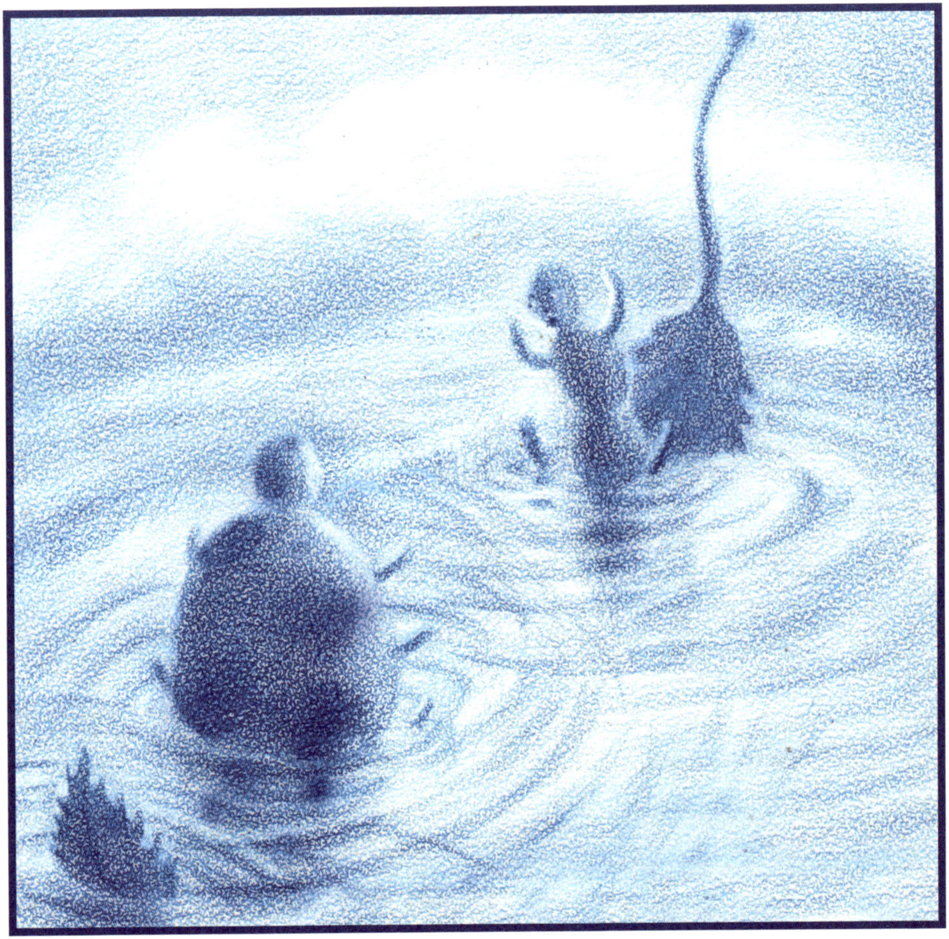

Why is it that when it is breezy
some land bugs think swimming is easy?
Their thoughts of flotation
breed miscalculation,
and their watery graves make us queasy.

The honey bee jounces a petal.
   Unsuccessful at first, he won't settle
      for work that's not done,
         so landing on one,
            he reveals pollinigerous mettle.

Where this spider's web
stores what's collected—
all its food—
is a pantry perfected.

It's so spacious
and sticky,
but as shelter
it's tricky:

its homeowner's not
well protected.

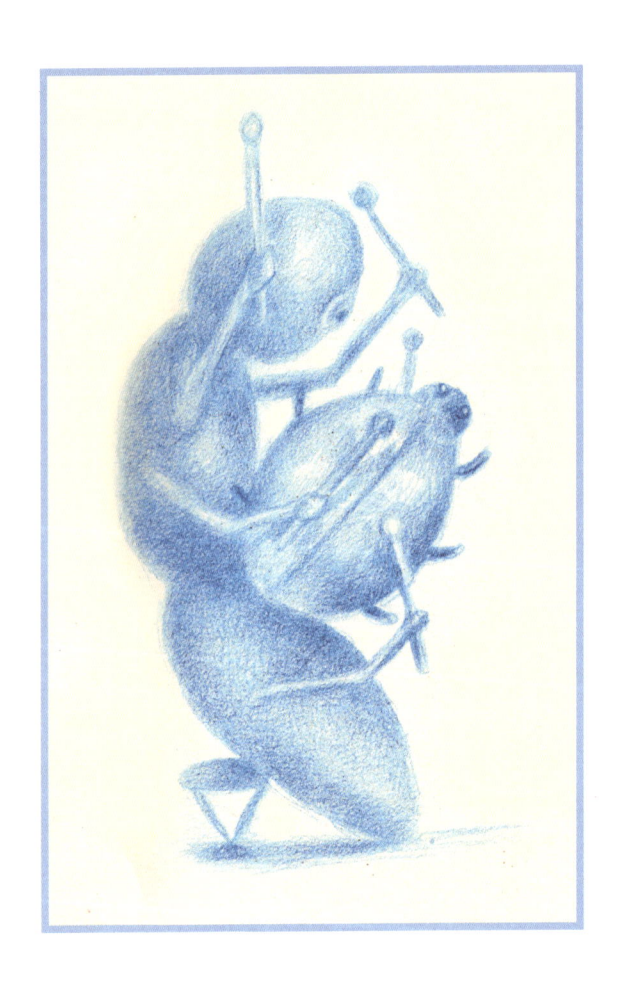

Their coat-of-arms
bugs us;
they "stink."
Attracted to lights,
counter, sink,
they dive-bomb,
careen;
scores cling
to the screen.
We flick 'em,
enjoying their "tink."

They flit, dip, and glide in the summers,
wearing flamboyant garb like the Mummers.
If only we'd capture a bit of that rapture
of their wings dancing to their own drummers!

Assassin bugs, kind of Macbeth-ish
delight in foul play (it's their fetish).
Moving in for a kill
is all part of the thrill
of them granting their bug-brothers' death wish.

Did some wanderlust lead to your quest?
All alone, you're our lucky houseguest,
but if we spot others
(say a few hundred brothers),
we'll annihilate you and your nest.

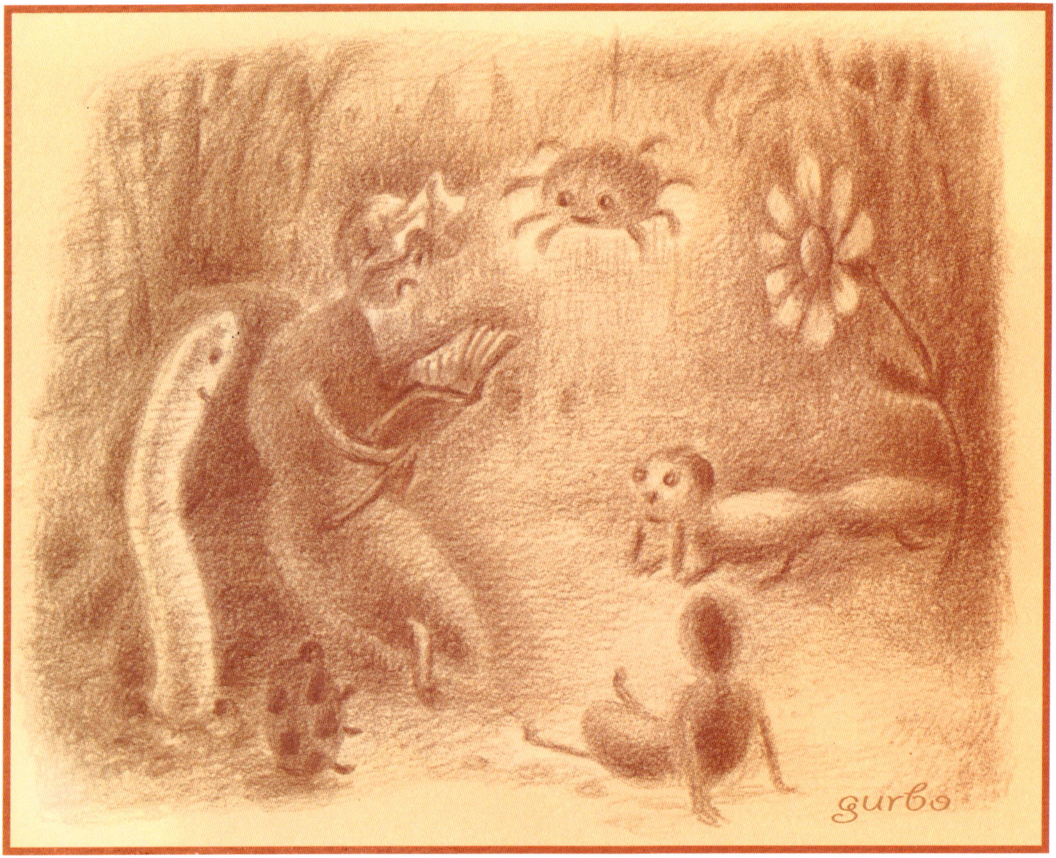
gurbo

A tiny brown spider is resting
on webs that never need testing.
She catches bad bugs,
those plant-bullies, thugs
who'll soon be what she's digesting.

When an ant will not work like his brothers
and insists that he, given his druthers,
should remain in one spot
to think his own thought,
he'll be ostracized by all the others.

By a garbage can
down
a back alley
Is where army ants
rant
at a rally.
What's these
legionnaires'
mission?
It's colonial
fission
since their
masses are too
great to tally.

Little Jesus bugs,
ever satirical,
show walking on water's
no miracle.
They stride
with such ease
and do
as they please.
Why can't
we be
equally spiritual?

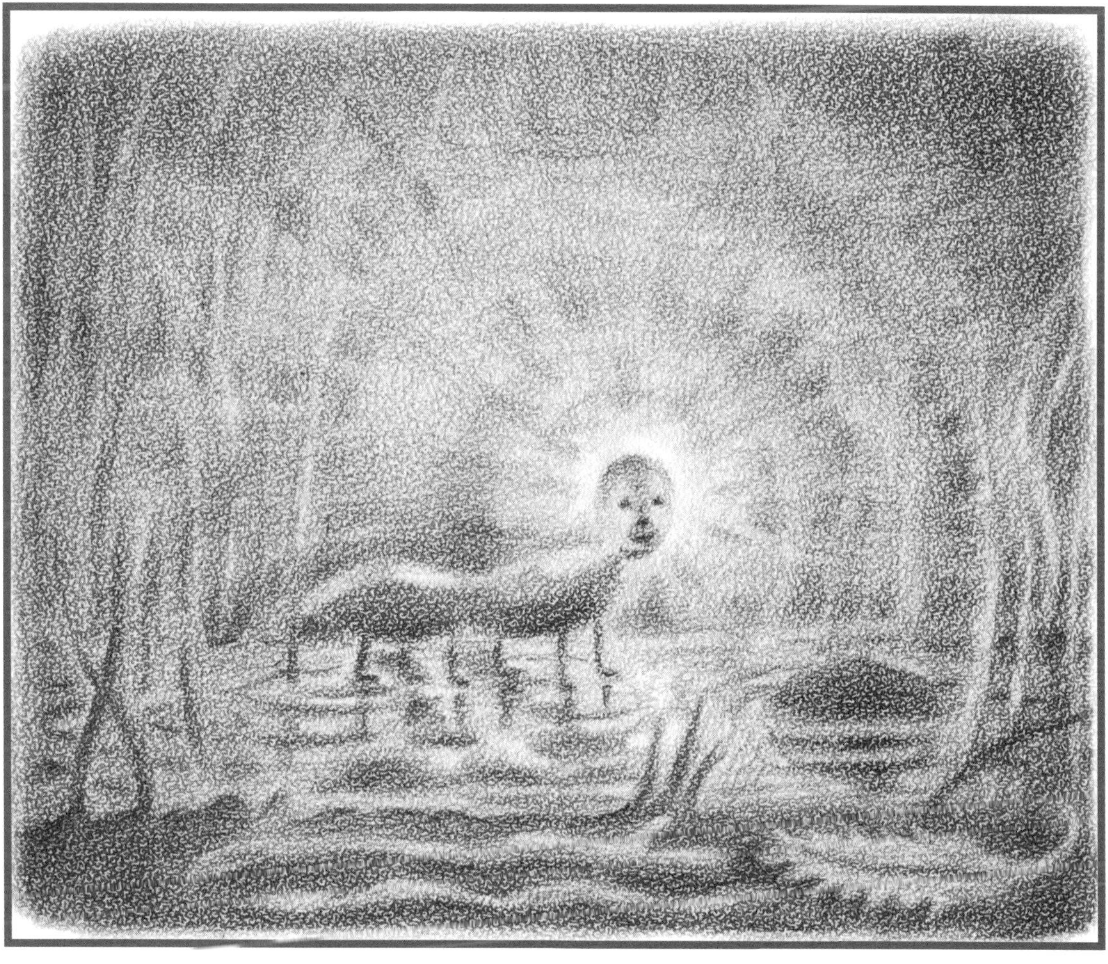

This centipede's legs run and shine
like silk that's propelled in a line.
She darts toward the drain
to avoid all the pain
of my sole (proof we both lack a spine).

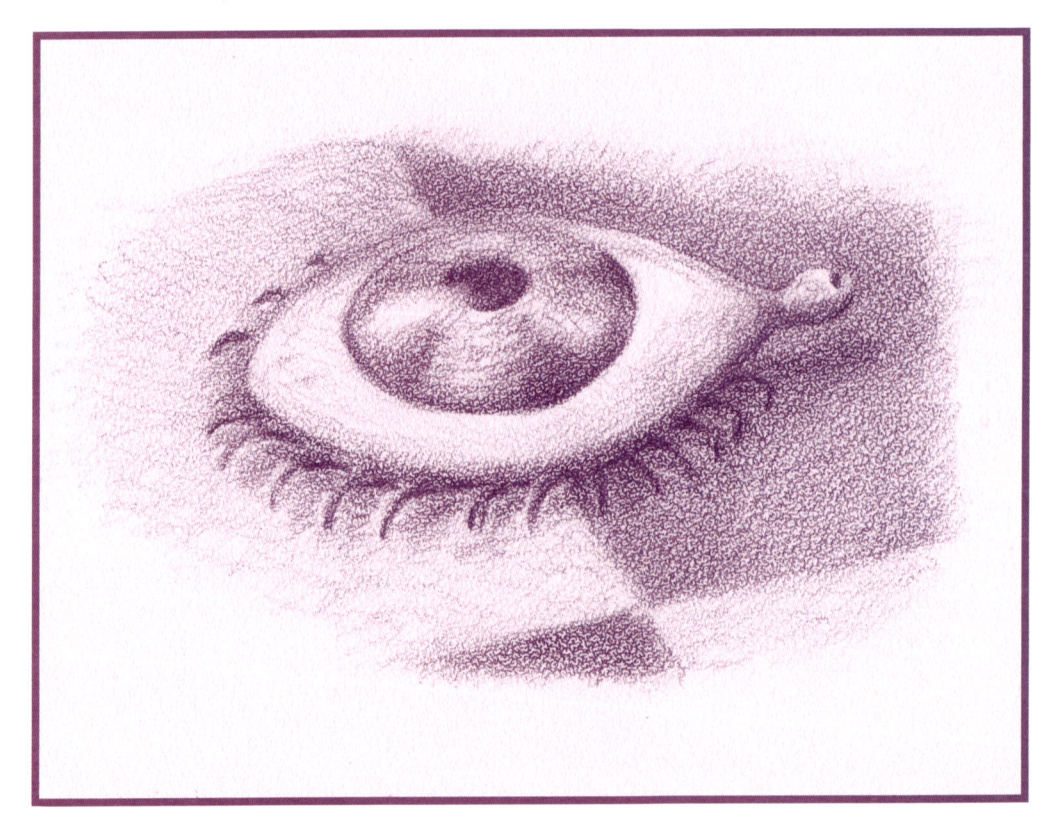

Odiferous ants are intense.
Through our kitchen they've followed the scents.
Their queen gave them orders,
"March! Infiltrate borders.
Your victory's my eminence!"

When it's wet, what a day for a date
to romance one's own self—one's soul mate.
This singular crawl?
A hermaphrodite's ball!
If dismembered, just regenerate.

This plant-clinging
aphid's
not feeding!

And a lunch date
is not what
she's needing.

There are no males for
dating,
and she's not up
for mating.

Perhaps this leaf's
intriguing
reading?

When mating at dusk, they're one ghost.
By themselves they're annoying at most.
Why do they insist
near my face to persist
when I'm trying to make a good toast?

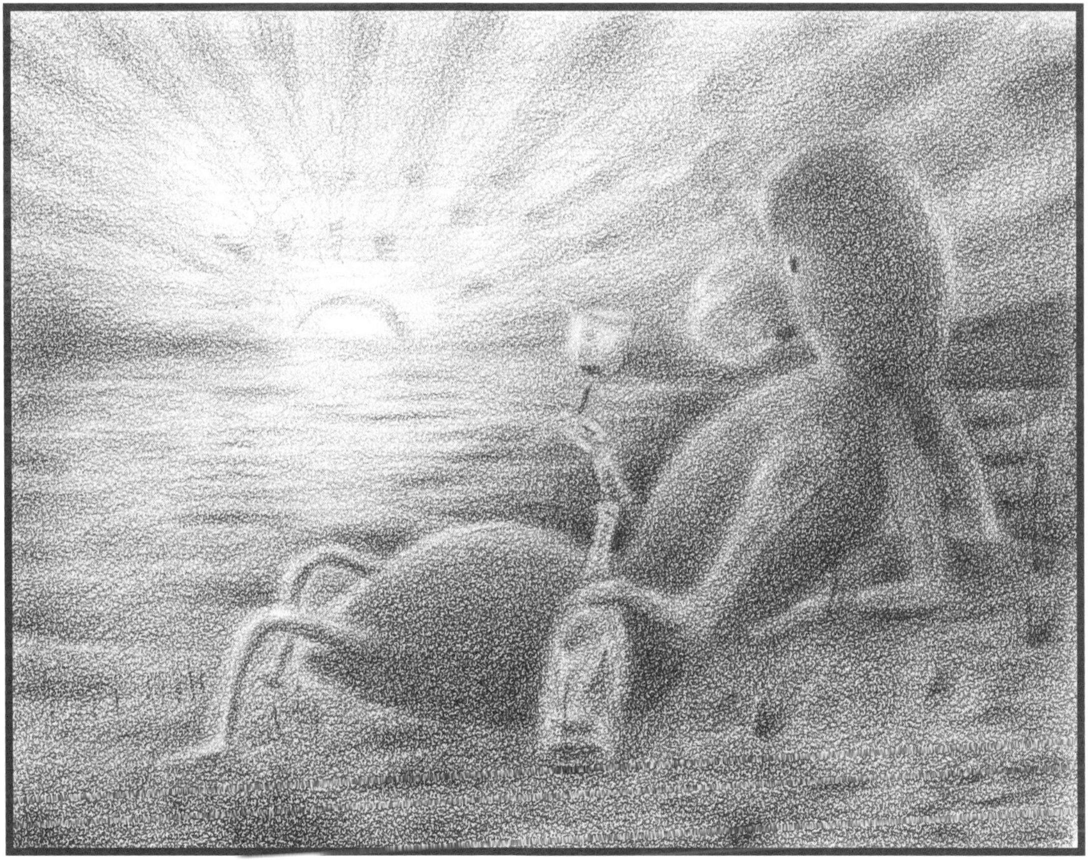